COSTA RICA 2016 HUMAN RIGHTS REPORT

EXECUTIVE SUMMARY

Costa Rica is a constitutional republic governed by a president and a unicameral legislative assembly directly elected in multiparty elections every four years. In April 2014 voters elected Luis Guillermo Solis of the Citizen Action Party (PAC) during a second round of elections. In simultaneous legislative elections in 2014, the PAC, Broad Front, and Social Christian Unity Party gained seats and formed a coalition that gave them control of the legislature. The National Liberation Party (PLN) gained the largest number of seats but did not achieve the required majority. In May the PLN and other opposition parties formed a bloc that gave them control of the legislature. All elections were generally considered free and fair.

Civilian authorities maintained effective control over the security forces.

Principal human rights abuses included overcrowded prisons, discrimination based on sexual orientation and gender identity, and infringement on the rights of indigenous people.

Other human rights concerns included trafficking in persons, particularly sex trafficking of children. Domestic violence against women and children was also an area of societal concern.

The government investigated and prosecuted officials who committed abuses.

Section 1. Respect for the Integrity of the Person, Including Freedom from:

a. Arbitrary Deprivation of Life and other Unlawful or Politically Motivated Killings

There were no reports that the government or its agents committed arbitrary or unlawful killings. The Inspection Tribunal of the Judicial Branch acquitted nine Judicial Investigative Organization (OIJ) officers of responsibility for the death of an OIJ officer who died during an unauthorized training exercise in May 2015.

b. Disappearance

There were no reports of politically motivated disappearances.

c. Torture and Other Cruel, Inhuman, or Degrading Treatment or Punishment

The constitution prohibits such practices. The Ombudsman's Office received 107 complaints of police abuse, arbitrary detention, torture, and other inhuman or degrading treatment during the first six months of the year. Abuse by prison police was a recurring complaint, according to the Ombudsman's Office, but very few of the accusers followed through and registered their complaints with the authorities. The government investigated, prosecuted, and punished police responsible for confirmed cases of abuse.

Prison and Detention Center Conditions

Prison conditions were harsh due to gross overcrowding, inadequate sanitary conditions, difficulties obtaining medical care, and violence among prisoners.

Physical Conditions: The prison population exceeded the designed capacity of prisons by 41 percent as of June. Prison overcrowding made security and control difficult and contributed to health problems. Poor conditions included inadequate space for resting, deteriorated mattresses on the floor, and inadequate access to health services. Illegal narcotics were readily available in the prisons, and drug abuse was common. The Ombudsman's Office recorded 76 complaints of deficient conditions in prisons, including the migrant detention centers, during the first six months of the year. The Ministry of Justice was responsible for the prison system, while the Immigration Office ran the facility holding illegal migrants until they were deported or regularized their immigration status.

As of June 30, the San Sebastian, Gerardo Rodriguez, La Reforma, San Rafael, San Carlos, Pococi, Puntarenas, Liberia, Perez Zeledon, Cartago, and Centro Adulto Joven (at La Reforma) prisons remained overcrowded, with the population in pretrial detention experiencing the most overcrowding. Authorities held male pretrial detainees with convicted prisoners on occasion. In San Sebastian, where most prisoners in pretrial detention were held, 1,281 prisoners lived in unsanitary conditions in a facility with a planned capacity of 668. On April 5, the Ministry of Justice freed 380 prisoners from the Gerardo Rodriguez prison and included them in a prison alternative program after a judge on March 17 ordered the ministry to relocate prisoners to reduce overcrowding. On July 20, also to reduce overcrowding, a judge issued a resolution ordering authorities to close the San Sebastian prison over a period of 18 months. On August 4, to reduce overcrowding a judge ordered authorities either to transfer 200 prisoners from La

Reforma prison to other prisons or to include them in an alternative program where they are required to spend only some nights in prison.

The detention center for undocumented migrants in Hatillo, a suburb of San Jose, was poorly ventilated and overcrowded at times, and it had no recreation area. The Office of the UN High Commissioner for Refugees (UNHCR) and the government ombudsman monitored detention conditions, with UNHCR visiting monthly and the ombudsman preparing annual reports.

Security and administrative staffing were insufficient to care for the needs of prisoners, including ensuring their personal safety. The Ministry of Justice's Social Adaptation Division reported 17 deaths in closed regime centers from January to April. Four of these deaths were homicides and two were suicides; the remainder were from natural causes.

Administration: Authorities permitted prisoners and detainees to submit complaints to authorities without censorship and request investigation of credible allegations of inhuman conditions. If complaints were not processed, prisoners could submit them to the Ombudsman's Office, which investigated all complaints at an administrative level. The Ombudsman's Office, through the national prevention mechanism against torture, periodically inspected all detention centers.

Independent Monitoring: The government permitted independent monitoring of prison conditions by international and local human rights observers, including representatives from the Ombudsman's Office. Human rights observers could speak to prisoners and prison employees in confidence and without the presence of prison staff or other third parties.

Improvements: On April 29, the Ministry of Justice inaugurated a new prison module at the Pococi prison, a Quonset-type steel-framed building with tin roofing and siding; however, prisoners complained of high temperature conditions in the facility. In August the Ministry of Justice reported maintenance and minor repairs in all of the country's prison centers.

d. Arbitrary Arrest or Detention

The constitution prohibits arbitrary arrest and detention, and the government generally observed these prohibitions.

Role of the Police and Security Apparatus

The country has no military forces. Civilian authorities maintained effective control over the 13 agencies that have law enforcement components, including the judicial branch's Judicial Investigative Organization. The Ministry of Public Security is responsible for the uniformed police force, drug control police, border police, air wing, and coast guard. The Immigration Office of the Ministry of Interior is responsible for the immigration police. The Ministry of Public Works and Transportation supervises the traffic police, the Ministry of Environment supervises park police, and the Ministry of Justice manages the penitentiary police. Several municipalities manage municipal police forces. The government has effective mechanisms to investigate and punish abuse and corruption. There were no reports of impunity involving the security forces during the year. The number of licensed private security services was significantly greater than the number of police (27,625 agents compared to 13,459 uniformed police officers). There were no reports of impunity involving the private security forces during the year.

Arrest Procedures and Treatment of Detainees

The law requires issuance of judicial warrants before making arrests, except where probable cause is evident to the arresting officer. The law entitles a detainee to a judicial determination of the legality of detention during arraignment before a judge within 24 hours of arrest. The law provides for the right to post bail and prompt access to an attorney and family members. Authorities generally observed these rights. Indigent persons have access to a public attorney at government expense. Those without sufficient personal funds are also able to use the services of a public defender. With judicial authorization, authorities may hold a suspect incommunicado for 48 hours after arrest or, under special circumstances, for up to 10 days. Special circumstances include cases in which pretrial detention previously was ordered and there is reason to believe a suspect may reach an agreement with accomplices or may obstruct the investigation. Suspects were allowed access to attorneys immediately before submitting statements before a judge. Authorities promptly informed suspects of any offenses under investigation. Habeas corpus provides legal protection for citizens against threats from police; it also requires judges to give a clear explanation of the legal basis for detention of and evidence against a suspect.

Pretrial Detention: A criminal court may hold suspects in pretrial detention for up to one year, and the court of appeals may extend this period to two years in especially complex cases. The law requires a court review every three months of cases of suspects in pretrial detention to determine the appropriateness of continued detention. If a judge declares a case is related to organized crime, special procedural rules require that the period of pretrial detention not exceed 24 months (although the court of appeals may grant one extension not to exceed an additional 12 months). Authorities frequently used pretrial detention. According to the Ministry of Justice, as of March 31, persons in pretrial detention constituted approximately 18 percent of the prison population. In some cases delays were due to pending criminal investigations and lengthy legal procedures. In other cases the delays were a result of court backlogs.

<u>Detainee's Ability to Challenge Lawfulness of Detention before a Court</u>: Persons arrested or detained, regardless of whether on criminal or other grounds, are entitled to challenge in court the legal basis or arbitrary nature of their detention and obtain prompt release and compensation if found to have been unlawfully detained.

e. Denial of Fair Public Trial

The constitution provides for an independent judiciary, and the government generally respected judicial independence. The legal system faced many challenges, including significant delays in the adjudication of criminal cases and civil disputes and a growing workload.

Trial Procedures

The constitution and law provide for the right to a fair public trial, and an independent judiciary generally enforced this right.

All defendants have the right to the presumption of innocence, to be informed promptly and in detail of the charges, and to trial without undue delay. All trials, except those that include juvenile defendants, are public. Trials that involve victims or witnesses who are minors are closed during the portion of the trial in which the minor is called to testify. Defendants have the right to be present during trial and communicate with an attorney of choice in a timely manner, or to have one provided at public expense. Defendants enjoy the right to adequate time and facilities to prepare a defense and free interpretation as necessary from the moment charged through all appeals. The law provides detainees and attorneys access to government-held evidence, and during the trial defendants can confront prosecution or plaintiff witnesses and present witnesses and evidence on their own behalf. Defendants have the right not to be compelled to testify or confess guilt. Defendants, if convicted, have the right to appeal. The law extends these rights to all defendants, citizens and noncitizens alike. Fast-track courts, which prosecute cases when suspects are arrested on the spot for alleged transgressions, provide the same protections and rights as other courts.

Political Prisoners and Detainees

There were no reports of political prisoners or detainees.

Civil Judicial Procedures and Remedies

An independent and impartial judiciary presides over lawsuits in civil matters, including human rights violations. Administrative and judicial remedies for alleged wrongs are available to the public. Individuals and organizations may appeal adverse domestic decisions to regional human rights bodies.

f. Arbitrary or Unlawful Interference with Privacy, Family, Home, or Correspondence

The constitution prohibits such actions, and there were no reports the government failed to respect these prohibitions.

Section 2. Respect for Civil Liberties, Including:

a. Freedom of Speech and Press

The constitution provides for freedom of speech and press, and the government generally respected these rights. An independent press, an effective judiciary, and a functioning democratic political system combined to promote freedom of speech and press.

Censorship or Content Restrictions: On July 11, a daily newspaper complained of pressures from a state-owned bank for publishing critical articles. The bank withdrew official advertising from the newspaper allegedly to influence the newspaper's content.

Internet Freedom

The government did not restrict or disrupt access to the internet or censor online content, and there were no credible reports the government monitored private communications without appropriate legal authority. The International

Telecommunication Union reported that in 2015, 60 percent of individuals used the internet and 60 percent of households had internet access.

Academic Freedom and Cultural Events

There were no government restrictions on academic freedom or cultural events.

b. Freedom of Peaceful Assembly and Association

The constitution provides for the freedoms of assembly and association, and the government generally respected these rights in practice.

c. Freedom of Religion

See the Department of State's *International Religious Freedom Report* at www.state.gov/religiousfreedomreport/.

d. Freedom of Movement, Internally Displaced Persons, Protection of Refugees, and Stateless Persons

The constitution and law provide for freedom of internal movement, foreign travel, emigration, and repatriation, and the government generally respected these rights. The government cooperated with UNHCR and other humanitarian organizations in providing protection and assistance to refugees, asylum seekers, stateless persons, or other persons of concern.

Protection of Refugees

Access to Asylum: The law provides for the granting of asylum or refugee status, and the government has an established system for providing protection to refugees. The law requires authorities to process the claims within three months of receipt, but decisions took an average of 10 months.

The number of persons seeking asylum increased nearly 300 percent over previous years. The refugee unit received 2,075 asylum applications from January to June, mainly from El Salvador and Colombia, compared with 2,198 in all of 2015 and 1,373 in all of 2014.

Employment: Refugee regulations provide asylum seekers an opportunity to obtain work permits if they have to wait beyond the three months the law allows for a decision on their asylum claim. Few asylum seekers took advantage of this right, largely because they were unaware of their eligibility. The refugee unit failed to process claims in a timely manner or effectively educate employers about this right. The Appeals Tribunal, which adjudicates all migration appeals, as of August had a backlog of 1,000 cases. The tribunal estimated it could resolve these cases by December by significantly increasing staff with additional funding from UNHCR, but since it anticipated hundreds of new cases in coming months, it expected a reduced backlog to remain.

Access to Basic Services: By law asylum seekers and refugees have access to public services and social welfare programs, but access was often hampered by lack of knowledge about their status in the country and feelings of xenophobia among some service providers. For example, asylum seekers without employers (who constituted the majority of asylum seekers) faced restrictions when enrolling voluntarily as independent workers in the public health system.

Asylum seekers received provisional refugee status documents legalizing their status after appearing for an interview with the General Directorate of Immigration, for which the estimated wait time was approximately two months. Provisional refugee ID cards do not resemble other Costa Rican identity documents, so while government authorities generally accepted them, many Costa Rican citizens did not. Upon receiving refugee status, which typically took another nine months, refugees could obtain an identity document similar to those used by nationals at a cost of 37,400 colones ($68), renewable every two years.

Durable Solutions: In July the government agreed to a "Protection Transfer Arrangement" in coordination with UNHCR and the International Organization for Migration for refugee resettlement in third countries. The government was committed to local integration of refugees both legally and socially and to facilitating their naturalization process. In the September Leaders' Summit on Refugees at the United Nations, President Solis highlighted commitments by the government to improve processing and conditions for refugees.

Temporary Protection: There were no programs for temporary protection beyond refugee status. Due to low recognition rates (approximately 26 percent of applicants received asylum during the first six months of the year), UNHCR had to consider a number of rejected asylum seekers as persons in need of international protection. UNHCR provided support and access to integration programs to individuals still pursuing adjudication and appeals. The individuals requesting refugee status were mainly from El Salvador, Colombia, and Venezuela; the majority were male adults and extended families.

Stateless Persons

The Ministry of Foreign Affairs cooperated with UNHCR efforts on statelessness with indigenous populations and reported no cases of the recognition of one person's status as stateless during the first six months of the year. There were no reports of stateless persons who were also refugees. There continued to be problems of statelessness of indigenous children and children of seasonal workers in the border areas with Panama and Nicaragua derived from the difficulties linked to birth registrations. Members of the Ngobe-Bugle indigenous group from Panama often worked on Costa Rican plantations and occasionally gave birth there. In these cases parents did not register Ngobe-Bugle children as Costa Rican citizens at birth because they did not think it necessary, although the children lacked registration in Panama as well. Approximately 1,200 children were affected. Government authorities worked together with UNHCR on a program of birth registration and provision of identification documents to stateless persons known as "Chiriticos." Mobile teams went to remote coffee-growing areas for case identification and registration. As of June authorities identified 1,783 individuals, confirmed the nationality of 748, registered 79, and began the registration process for 119 individuals.

Section 3. Freedom to Participate in the Political Process

The constitution and laws provide citizens the ability to choose their government in free and fair periodic elections held by secret ballot and based on universal and equal suffrage.

Elections and Political Participation

Recent Elections: In April 2014 voters elected PAC's Luis Guillermo Solis president during a second round of elections, after no candidate achieved 40 percent of the first-round vote. Presidential and legislative elections are simultaneous. In legislative elections the National Liberation Party gained the most seats, but three parties--the PAC, Broad Front, and Social Christian Unity Party (PUSC)--gained enough seats in the 57-member legislative assembly to form a coalition that gave them control of the legislature in 2014. On May 1, PLN and other opposition parties formed a bloc that gave them control of the legislature. In municipal elections on February 7, PLN and PUSC parties gained control of 62 of

81 municipalities. Observers considered the elections generally free and fair. The Organization of American States team that observed the elections noted that for the first time the election process included citizens voting from abroad.

<u>Participation of Women and Minorities</u>: Women and persons of African descent were represented in government, but indigenous people were not. On May 23, the supreme elections tribunal imposed strict gender quotas for political parties, reaffirming existing regulations that all political parties must guarantee gender parity across their electoral slates and confirming that gender parity has to extend vertically. The electoral code requires that a minimum of 50 percent of candidates for elective office be women, with their names placed alternately with men on the ballots by party slate.

Section 4. Corruption and Lack of Transparency in Government

The law provides criminal penalties for corruption by officials, and the government generally implemented the law effectively. There were numerous reports of government corruption during the year.

<u>Corruption</u>: On March 15, the labor minister resigned for violating a code of ethics that he had helped to promote, after he hired his niece at the ministry. On August 10, a former OIJ secretary general was sentenced to 12 years in prison for embezzlement charges from 2009.

<u>Financial Disclosure</u>: Public officials are subject to financial disclosure laws that require senior officials to submit sworn declarations of income, assets, and liabilities. The law requires income and asset disclosure by appointed and elected officials. The content of the declarations is not made available to the public. The law stipulates administrative sanctions for noncompliance and identifies which assets, liabilities, and interests public officials must declare. Officials are required to file a declaration annually and upon entering and leaving office.

<u>Public Access to Information</u>: The law provides for public access to government information, and the government generally implemented the law effectively, providing access for citizens and noncitizens, including foreign media. Authorities have 10 days to disclose or respond to a request for access. There are no processing fees or sanctions for noncompliance, although requesters can file a petition if their request is denied. Government institutions published reports that detailed their activities during the year. The Public Ethics Solicitor's Office provided regular training to public employees on public access to information. The

Ombudsman's Office operated a webpage dedicated to enhancing transparency by improving citizens' access to public information.

Section 5. Governmental Attitude Regarding International and Nongovernmental Investigation of Alleged Violations of Human Rights

A number of domestic and international human rights groups generally operated without government restriction, investigating and publishing their findings on human rights cases. Government officials were often cooperative and responsive to their views.

Government Human Rights Bodies: The Ombudsman's Office reviews government action or inaction that affects citizens' rights and interests. The ombudsman is accountable to the legislative assembly, which appoints the person to a four-year term and funds office operations. The ombudsman participates in the drafting and approval of legislation, promotes good administration and transparency, and reports annually to the legislative assembly with nonbinding recommendations. A special committee of the legislative assembly studies and reports on problems relating to the violation of human rights, and it also reviews bills relating to human rights and international humanitarian law.

Section 6. Discrimination, Societal Abuses, and Trafficking in Persons

Women

Rape and Domestic Violence: The law criminalizes rape, including spousal rape and domestic violence, and provides penalties from 10 to 18 years in prison for rape. The length of the sentence depends on the victim's age and other factors, such as the assailant's use of violence or position of influence over the victim. The judicial branch generally enforced the law. According to a local nongovernmental organization, rape was underreported due to fear of retribution, further violence, social stigma, or lack of trust in the judicial system.

According to the National Institute of Women (INAMU), the rape law applies to spousal rape, although such cases were much more difficult to prove. The judicial branch and the social security system continued to implement a program for collecting physical evidence in cases of rape so that victims could receive immediate attention. The program also provided training to emergency services staff. Four locations in the country, besides the judicial forensic clinic, had rape kits to collect and analyze physical evidence for use in prosecutions. In May the judicial branch and the social security system organized a weeklong training event focusing on capacity building for officials responding to victims of sexual violence; the audience consisted of judges, prosecutors, investigators, medical professionals, and social workers from across the country.

The government continued to identify domestic violence against women and children as a serious and growing societal problem. The judicial branch reported that 39 women died from gender-based violence (including 28 femicides) during 2015. INAMU reported that 12 women were killed (including seven femicides) during the first six months of the year. The law prohibits domestic violence and provides measures for the protection of domestic violence victims. Criminal penalties range from 10 to 100 days in prison for aggravated threats and up to 35 years in prison for aggravated homicide, including a sentence of 20 to 35 years for persons who kill their partners. If a domestic violence offender has no violent criminal record and is sentenced to fewer than three years' imprisonment, the law also provides for alternative sanctions, such as weekend detentions and assistance, including referrals for social services and rehabilitation. In 2015, according to the judicial branch's statistics office, authorities opened 18,693 cases of domestic violence throughout the country, but only 859 cases were tried and 517 persons sentenced for crimes of violence against women, including six homicides. According to the Attorney General's Office, not all cases originated from a report from a victim, and frequently victims refused to continue with the legal process.

INAMU assisted women and their children who were victims of domestic violence in its regional office in San Jose and in three other specialized centers and temporary shelters. INAMU maintained a domestic abuse hotline connected to the 911 emergency telephone system and provided counseling and protection to women and their children.

The public prosecutor, police, and ombudsman have offices dedicated to addressing domestic violence.

Sexual Harassment: The law prohibits sexual harassment in the workplace and educational institutions, and the Ministry of Labor and Social Security generally enforced this prohibition. The law imposes penalties ranging from a letter of reprimand to dismissal, with more serious incidents subject to criminal prosecution. The Ombudsman's Office received 116 complaints of sexual harassment in the workplace between January and June. INAMU reported and assisted in investigating 18 cases of sexual harassment.

<u>Reproductive Rights</u>: Couples and individuals have the right to decide the number, spacing, and timing of children; to manage their reproductive health; and to have access to the information and means to do so, free from discrimination, coercion, or violence. In 2015 the president signed an executive order legalizing in-vitro fertilization to comply with the 2012 Inter-American Court of Human Rights (IACHR) order to reinstate women's right to undergo the procedure. In February the Supreme Court struck down the executive order, but in March the IACHR upheld it, and the order went into effect legalizing in-vitro fertilization.

<u>Discrimination</u>: Women enjoy the same legal status and rights as men. The law prohibits discrimination against women and obligates the government to promote political, economic, social, and cultural equality. The government maintained offices for gender-related problems in most ministries. The Ministry of Labor is responsible for investigating allegations of gender discrimination. The law requires women and men receive equal pay for equal work. In 2014 the National Institute of Statistics and Census (INEC) estimated earnings for women were 92 percent of earned income for men. INAMU enhanced women's economic empowerment through programs on employment quality, support networks, seed capital, and entrepreneurship.

Children

<u>Birth Registration</u>: Citizenship is obtained from birth within the country's territory or can be derived if either parent is Costa Rican. There were occasional problems encountered in the registration at birth of children born of migrant parents. Birth registration was not always automatic, and migrant children were especially at risk of statelessness since they did not have access to legal documents to establish their identity if their parents did not seek birth registration for them.

<u>Child Abuse</u>: Abuse of children continued to be a problem. The autonomous National Institute for Children (PANI) reported violence against children and adolescents continued to be a concern, with 10,889 cases from January to June. Traditional attitudes and the inclination to treat sexual and psychological abuse as misdemeanors hampered legal proceedings against persons accused of committing crimes against children. PANI implemented awareness campaigns to prevent abuse, humiliating treatment, neglect, and commercial sexual exploitation. The Ombudsman's Office considered efforts by public institutions to prevent violence and promote positive parenting were unsuccessful or insufficient.

<u>Early and Forced Marriage</u>: The minimum legal age of marriage is 18, or 15 with parental consent.

<u>Sexual Exploitation of Children</u>: The minimum age of consensual sex is 15 years. The law criminalizes the commercial sexual exploitation of children and provides sentences of up to 16 years in prison for violations. The law provides for sentences of two to 10 years in prison for statutory rape and three to eight years in prison for child pornography. Sentences are lengthier in aggravated circumstances; for example, rape involving physical violence or a victim under the age of 13 is punishable by 10 to 16 years' imprisonment. The government, security officials, and child advocacy organizations acknowledged that commercial sexual exploitation of children was a serious problem. From January to June, PANI reported 21 cases of commercial sexual exploitation of minors. PANI belongs to the executive branch and works with a different database, which includes all complaints filed of alleged cases, than the one for the judicial branch, which includes prosecuted cases only. The government identified child sex tourism as a serious problem.

<u>International Child Abductions</u>: The country is a party to the 1980 Hague Convention on the Civil Aspects of International Child Abduction. See the Department of State's *Annual Report on International Parental Child Abduction* at travel.state.gov/content/childabduction/en/legal/compliance.html.

Anti-Semitism

The Jewish Zionist Center estimated there were 3,000 Jews in the country. There were no reports of anti-Semitic acts.

Trafficking in Persons

See the Department of State's *Trafficking in Persons Report* at www.state.gov/j/tip/rls/tiprpt/.

Persons with Disabilities

The constitution and law prohibit discrimination against persons with physical, sensory, intellectual, or mental disabilities in employment, education, air travel and other transportation, access to health care, the judicial system, or the provision of other state services; however, the government did not effectively enforce the law. Discriminatory practices were reported in access to education, employment, information, public buildings, and transportation. The law establishes a clear right to employment for persons with disabilities and sets a hiring quota of 5 percent of vacant positions in the public sector. The government began registering eligible candidates in May, according to the National Council of Disabled Persons.

Although the law mandates access to buildings for persons with disabilities, the government did not enforce this provision, and many buildings remained inaccessible to persons with disabilities. Both the government policy on education and the national plan for higher education establish the right to education for students with special needs. The Ministry of Education operated a program for persons with disabilities that provided support services to students with disabilities in both mainstream and special education systems.

A political party, Accessibility without Exclusion, represented the interests of persons with disabilities and held one seat in the legislative assembly. The Supreme Elections Tribunal took measures (voting procedures, facilities, materials, and trained personnel) to provide for fully accessible elections for all persons with disabilities.

National/Racial/Ethnic Minorities

In 2015 INEC reported that 38 percent of inhabitants in the heavily Afro-descendant Atlantic region lived in poverty, compared with the national average of 22 percent. The Atlantic region had one of the country's highest rates of unemployment (12 percent in 2015) and crime (22.4 homicides per 100,000 inhabitants in 2015, or double the national average of 11.5 homicides per 100,000 inhabitants). Lack of government investment in infrastructure contributed to Limon, a province with twice the national average of Afro-descendant population, being one of the least developed areas of the country.

The constitution establishes that the country is a multiethnic and multicultural nation. According to the Ombudsman's Office, however, the country lacked an adequate legal framework to ensure the right mechanisms to combat discrimination, facilitate the adoption of affirmative action for individuals who suffer discrimination, and establish sanctions for those who commit discriminatory acts.

There were sporadic reports of discrimination, including racial/ethnic discrimination, as well as labor discrimination, usually directed against Nicaraguans. The Ombudsman's Office recorded five complaints of racial/ethnic discrimination, including denial, deficiency, or mistreatment in health-care services as well as restriction of freedom of association, during the first six months of the year. Two cases against judicial prosecutors accused of racial slurs against coworkers were first made public in February; one prosecutor was sentenced to a one-month suspension, while the other case remained under investigation.

Indigenous People

Land ownership continued to be a problem in most indigenous territories. Violent incidents at the Bribri Salitre and Cabagra reservations over land disputes between indigenous inhabitants and nonindigenous reemerged during the year. The law protects reserve land as the collective, nontransferable property in 24 indigenous territories; however, 38 percent of that land was in nonindigenous hands. On April 10, during an official visit to the reservations, government authorities stated they were committed to improving security and streamlining the provision of assistance from public institutions.

On March 15, the government issued an executive directive to begin the process of establishing a consultative mechanism with the indigenous peoples, and on April 13, the government announced it would conduct a series of workshops with leaders of the 24 indigenous territories.

Acts of Violence, Discrimination, and Other Abuses Based on Sexual Orientation and Gender Identity

The constitution establishes that all persons are equal before the law and no discrimination contrary to human dignity shall be practiced. Discrimination against persons based on sexual orientation and gender identity is prohibited by a series of executive orders and workplace policies but not by national laws. Transgender persons were able to change their gender on their identity documents through an administrative law judge's decision and later registration in the Civil Registry Office.

There were cases of discrimination against persons based on sexual orientation, ranging from employment, police abuse, and education to access to health-care services. Lesbian, gay, bisexual, transgender, and intersex (LGBTI) organizations operated freely and lobbied for legal reforms. In 2015 a family court recognized the first "gay common-law marriage," basing the decision on the 2013 youth law that includes a provision legalizing domestic partnership benefits only for persons between 18 and 35 years of age. The Constitutional Chamber of the Supreme

Court was studying a constitutional challenge against that provision of the youth law but as of August had not issued a ruling. A 2010 Supreme Court ruling stated that the decision on same-sex civil unions is a legislative one; at year's end, however, the legislative assembly had not passed legislation addressing that issue.

On March 3, two women who married filed a constitutionality complaint before the Supreme Court to prevent the annulment of their marriage, alleging a provision of the family law that prohibits same-sex unions is unconstitutional. The Civil Registry Office in 2015 filed a complaint against the two women, alleging this was an unlawful marriage because the registry had listed one of them as a man. The judicial inspection tribunal was investigating a judge who issued a ruling recognizing the first "gay common-law marriage."

In May the government reformed regulations applying to government employees and students to prohibit discrimination based on sexual orientation or gender identity and to extend bereavement leave benefits to include same-sex partners. In June the social security system approved a survivor pension for same-sex couples, complementing the 2014 regulation that extends insurance benefits to same-sex couples.

HIV and AIDS Social Stigma

Although the law prohibits discrimination based on HIV/AIDS in health care, housing, employment, and education, discrimination occurred. The Ombudsman's Office reported seven complaints of service denial, deficiencies, or mistreatment in health care toward HIV-positive patients during the first six months of the year.

Section 7. Worker Rights

a. Freedom of Association and the Right to Collective Bargaining

The law provides for the right of workers to form and join independent unions, bargain collectively, and conduct legal strikes, and the government respected these rights. The law prohibits antiunion discrimination and provides for reinstatement of workers fired for union activity. Restrictions on the minimum number of employees (12) needed to form a union may have hampered freedom of association in small enterprises. The law permits foreign workers to join unions but prohibits them from holding positions of authority within the unions, except for foreign workers who are married to citizens of the country and have legally resided in the country for at least five years. Unions must register, and the law provides a deadline of 15 days for authorities to reply to a registration request.

The legislative assembly established a minimum of 50 percent of employees in an enterprise in support of a strike for it to be legal; however, this law had not been implemented as of the end the year, and the minimum remained 60 percent. The law restricts the right to strike of workers in services designated as essential by the government, including in sectors such as oil refineries and ports that are not recognized as essential services under international standards. On January 25, President Solis signed into law a new labor procedural code (Law No. 9343) intended to streamline labor procedures in the courts, including those related to antiunion discrimination, and to reform provisions regarding freedom of association and trade union freedom in the courts. The new law enters into force 18 months after its publication (July 2017).

The law requires employers to initiate the bargaining process with a trade union if more than one-third of the total workforce, including union and nonunion members, requests collective bargaining, but the law also permits direct bargaining agreements with nonunionized workers. The law also permits the formation of "solidarity associations," which were often organized by employers and have legal status under the constitution. The law prohibits such associations from representing workers in collective bargaining negotiations or in any other way that assumes the functions or inhibits the formation of trade unions.

Although public-sector employees are permitted to bargain collectively, the Supreme Court held that some fringe benefits received by certain public employees were disproportionate and unreasonable, and it repealed sections of collective bargaining agreements between public-sector unions and government agencies, thus restricting this right in practice.

The government generally enforced applicable laws, although procedures were subject to lengthy delays and appeals. The law establishes administrative sanctions (fines and fees) for infractions. The amount of fines and fees is determined by the severity of the infraction and based on the minimum wage. Penalties were not sufficient to deter violations, since cases were resolved by a labor court through a lengthy process, not by the labor inspectorate. Labor inspectors are not allowed to impose fines directly because by law it is the exclusive competence of the judiciary. Concerns about slow proceedings in cases of antiunion discrimination continued to be a problem. The International Trade Union Confederation noted the reinstatement process for workers who were unfairly dismissed lasted approximately 2.5 years. Such delays in cases of antiunion discrimination were often due to numerous appeals.

Freedom of association and collective bargaining were generally respected. Labor unions asserted solidarity associations conducted negotiations, and employers sometimes required membership in a solidarity association as a condition for employment. Such associations, to the extent that they displaced trade unions, affected the independence of workers' organizations from employers' influence and infringed on the right to organize and bargain collectively. In recent years the International Labor Organization (ILO) reported an expansion of direct bargaining agreements between employers and nonunionized workers and noted its concern that the number of collective bargaining agreements in the private sector continued to be low when compared with a high number of direct agreements with nonunionized workers. The Labor Ministry conducted 10 working/mediation sessions to discuss complaints related to collective bargaining during the first six months of the year.

There were some instances of employers firing employees who attempted to unionize. The Ministry of Labor reported seven complaints of antiunion discrimination from January to July. There were reports some employers also preferred to use "flexible," or short-term, contracts, making it difficult for workers to organize and collectively bargain. Migrant workers in agriculture frequently were hired on short-term contracts (five months) through intermediaries, faced antiunion discrimination and challenges in organizing, and were often more vulnerable to labor exploitation.

The ILO noted there were no trade unions operating in the country's export-processing zones and identified the zones as a hostile environment for organizing. Labor unions asserted that efforts by workers in export-processing zones to organize were met with illegal employment termination, threats, and intimidation and that some employers maintained blacklists of workers identified as activists.

b. Prohibition of Forced or Compulsory Labor

The law prohibits forced or compulsory labor in cases that involve movement of the victim. The law establishes criminal penalties for trafficking in persons crimes, including forced labor--when they involve movement--with sentences of between six and 10 years in prison. The penalty is increased to between eight and 16 years if the crime involves aggravating circumstances. The Trafficking in Persons Prosecutor's Unit reported two investigations of trafficking in persons during the first six months of the year. One case was dismissed, and the second was under investigation. Penalties were generally sufficient to deter violations.

Also see the Department of State's *Trafficking in Persons Report* at www.state.gov/j/tip/rls/tiprpt/.

c. Prohibition of Child Labor and Minimum Age for Employment

The child and adolescence code prohibits labor of all children under the age of 15 without exceptions; it supersedes the minimum working age of 12 established in the labor code, which by year's end had not been amended to reflect this change. Adolescents between the ages of 15 and 18 may work a maximum of six hours daily and 36 hours weekly. The law prohibits night work and overtime for minors. The law prohibits children under the age of 18 from engaging in hazardous or unhealthy activities and specifies a list of hazardous occupations. The government generally enforced laws against child labor effectively in the formal sector but not in the informal sector.

Child labor occurred primarily in the informal economy, especially in the agricultural, commercial, and industrial sectors. The worst forms of child labor occurred in agriculture on small third-party farms in the formal sector and on family farms in the informal sector. In 2015 international organizations published an analysis of the government's 2011 National Household Survey, which indicated 8.8 percent of child laborers, or approximately 1,400 children ages 5-14, worked in coffee and 13.8 percent were engaged in cattle raising, including dairy. More recent national surveys showed a 65 percent decrease in the number of children ages 12 to 17 working in agriculture from 2011 to 2015 but did not provide the number of children in child labor in coffee and cattle. Forced child labor reportedly occurred in some service sectors, such as construction, fishing, street vending, and domestic service, and some children were subject to commercial sexual exploitation (see section 6, Children).

While the Ministry of Labor is responsible for enforcing and taking administrative actions (fines and fees) against possible violations of, or lack of compliance with, child labor laws, the Prosecutor's Office intervenes in cases regarding the worst forms of child labor. The amount of fines and fees is determined by the severity of the infraction and based on an equation derived from the minimum wage. Penalties were generally sufficient to deter violations.

The government continued to implement programming to eliminate illegal child labor and the worst forms of child labor by providing individual assistance through visits, interviews, and inspections to schools and workplaces. During the first six months of the year, the Labor Ministry detected and removed from employment 315 minors, 42 under 15, in hazardous jobs, referring them to government agencies for inclusion in social programs. The ministry reported that in the overwhelming majority of cases employers received warnings, and in the 42 cases that involved minors under 15, two employers were fined and one was referred to a labor court.

Also see the Department of Labor's *Findings on the Worst Forms of Child Labor* and *List of Goods Produced by Child Labor or Forced Labor* at www.dol.gov/ilab/reports/child-labor/findings/.

d. Discrimination with Respect to Employment or Occupation

The laws and regulations prohibit discrimination regarding race, color, sex, religion, political opinion, national origin or citizenship, social origin, disability, sexual orientation and/or gender identity, age, language, HIV-positive status, or other communicable diseases status. The government effectively enforced these laws and regulations, and penalties were sufficient to deter violations. The Labor Ministry reported 27 cases of discrimination during the first six months of the year. The ministry began incorporating a gender equality perspective into labor inspections to identify areas of vulnerability.

Discrimination in employment and occupation occurred with respect to persons with disabilities and the LGBTI population. Discrimination against migrant workers occurred. With regard to discrimination in employment or occupation, the Ombudsman's Office considered the most vulnerable sectors to be migrants, women with disabilities, Afro-descendants, and foreign domestic workers.

e. Acceptable Conditions of Work

The wage council of the Ministry of Labor sets the minimum wage scale for the public and private sectors twice a year. Monthly minimum wages for the private sector ranged from 172,610 colones ($314) for domestic workers to 619,204 colones ($1,126) for university graduates since January 1. According to INEC, in 2014 the poverty line was 105,976 colones ($193) in urban areas and 81,344 colones ($148) in rural areas. The national minimum wage applied to both Costa Rican and migrant workers. The law sets workday hours, overtime remuneration, days of rest, and annual vacation rights. Workers generally may work a maximum of eight hours a day or 48 hours weekly. All workers are entitled to one day of rest after six consecutive days of work and annual paid vacations. The law provides that workers be paid for overtime work at a rate 50 percent above their stipulated wage or salary. Although there is no statutory prohibition against compulsory overtime, the labor code stipulates the workday may not exceed 12 hours. Law 9095 covers labor exploitation as part of antitrafficking law and imposes penalties upon employers who exploit workers in conditions that are a "detriment to [a worker's] fundamental human rights" but that may not rise to the level of forced labor.

The government maintains a dedicated authority to enforce occupational safety and health (OSH) standards. The Labor Ministry's National Council of Occupational Health and Safety is a tripartite OSH regulatory authority with government, employer, and employee representation. According to labor organizations, the government did not enforce these standards effectively in either the formal or the informal sectors.

Workers can remove themselves from situations that endanger health or safety without jeopardizing their employment. According to the Labor Ministry, this is a responsibility shared by the employer and employee. The law assigns responsibility to the employer, including granting OSH officers access to workplaces, but it also authorizes workers to seek assistance from appropriate authorities (OSH or labor inspectors) for noncompliance with OSH workplace standards, including risks at work.

The Ministry of Labor's Inspection Directorate (DNI) is responsible for labor inspection, in collaboration with the Social Security Agency and the National Insurance Institute. The DNI employed 93 labor inspectors who investigated all types of labor violations. The number of inspectors was not sufficient to enforce compliance. According to the Ministry of Labor, inspections occurred both in response to complaints and at the initiative of inspectors. The DNI stated it could visit any employer, formal or informal, and inspections are always unannounced.

The Labor Ministry generally addressed complaints by sending inspection teams to investigate and coordinate with each other on follow-up actions. Inspectors cannot fine or sanction employers who do not comply with labor laws; rather, they investigate and refer noncompliance results to labor courts. The process of fining companies or compelling employers to pay back wages or overtime could take years.

The Ministry of Labor generally enforced minimum wages effectively in the San Jose area but was not as effective in enforcing the minimum wage laws in rural areas, particularly where large numbers of migrants were employed, and in the large informal sector, which comprises 41 percent of employment. The ministry publicly recognized that many workers, including in the formal sector, received less than the minimum wage. During the first six months of the year, the ministry conducted 1,405 visits to priority cantons with low levels of development in an attempt to assess and address their situation through DNI intervention.

The government continued to implement the campaign for minimum wage compliance. According to the ministry, 33 percent of the economically active population in the nonagricultural sector was in the informal economy. The Ministry of Labor, through the National Program in Support of the Microenterprise, provided technical assistance and access to credit for informal microentrepreneurs to improve productive and labor conditions in the informal economy.

Observers expressed concern about exploitative working conditions in fisheries, small businesses, and agricultural activities. Unions also reported systematic violations of labor rights and provisions concerning working conditions, overtime, and wages in the export-processing zones. Labor unions reported overtime pay violations, such as nonpayment of wages and mandatory overtime, were common in the private sector and particularly in export-processing zones. There were reports agricultural workers, particularly migrant laborers in the pineapple industry, worked in unsafe conditions, including exposure to hazardous chemicals without proper training. The national insurance company reported 61,203 cases of workplace-related illnesses and injuries and 19 workplace fatalities from January to June.